to Larry &
Lorna

No Other Business Here !

with Love, and
the usual stumbles
along the
way:.

John
1999

No Other Business Here

John Brandi Steve Sanfield

La Alameda Press :: Albuquerque

A bow of gratitude to the editors of
Exiled-in-America Press, Larkspur Press,
Tooth of Time Books, Tundra, and Yoo-Hoo Press
for first bringing some of these poems to light.

"A Contribution to the Understanding of the
Relationship Between Buddhism and Poetry"
was originally published in
American Zen: By a Guy Who Tried It
(Larkspur Press, 1994).

ISBN: 1-888809-17-5
Library of Congress #: 99-71682

First Edition

La Alameda Press
9636 Guadalupe Trail NW
Albuquerque, New Mexico 87114

If you come to a fork in the road, take it.
Yogi Berra

I'll play it first and
tell you what it is later.
Miles Davis

Three Liners, Unfettered

Writing in solitude has provided great exhilaration through the years, but undoubtedly my greatest joy has been in watching the detonation of traditional haiku into what poet/painter Paul Reps called "Zen Telegrams." These little missives, zipped back in forth in the mail, record moments of spark; a fleeting essence from a transient world made stationary; an unavoidable folly revealing a truth at the core of one's slapstick stumble.

Steve Sanfield and I have been communicating like this for decades—a way of keeping track of our lives: him in the piney Sierra Nevada canyons at the end of Lost River Road; me in the cottonwood flood-plain of the Rio Grande. Occasionally we pen those necessary long-winded letters, but the missives most relished are those unburdened by rant or lengthy epistles. Ones that arrive scrawled on postcards as three-line chuckles or uncanny wake-ups. Primal telegrams that bring us to the table over the distance. *Senryu* is the Japanese term for poems of the haiku form that reflect, not necessarily essences of the natural world, but situations of ordinary human concern. Over the years I've heard us refer to our work as "hoops," "twists" and "American haiku." Indeed, on close examination, the poems do fall somewhere between haiku and senryu.

No matter what the terminology, one thing remains essential: one must be careful not to slide into sentiment, metaphor, symbolism, prattle, ego or—worse—celebrating the obvious after rumination or reflection. Bashō put it this way:

> How admirable
> one who sees lightning flash
> and says not—how fleeting life!

If I stand back far enough I see two broken-shoed guys engaged in an age-old art of call and response. The Japanese call it *maekuzuke*, "connecting with previous verse." In this tradition the first verse (the "call") is a kind of general two-liner, to which the challenged poet comes back with an imagistic, often humorous three-liner (the "response"). But neither of these guys is Japanese, and never is there any notion of challenge or expectation of rebound. Their poems make no attempt to adhere to tradition. Neither is interested in poetry kept afloat by rules, contests or awards. Both write poetry to stay alive, to see where they've been, to give clearing for the next step.

Why do they proceed with this rapidly disappearing form of communication—licking stamps, addressing envelopes, dropping them in a local post office slot—or elbowing through crowds in Benares, Istanbul, Athens or Jakarta to the often impressive Bureau of Mails? The answer may be: little interest in electronic mail; no interest in a world full of aggressive resumé-waving careerists perfecting well-crafted prize-winning poetry; plenty of interest in quick, unfettered dazzles of surprise—often ungainly, sometimes beautiful—full of abandonment, precise in their communication. Finally, and most importantly, these guys lick their stamps and send their shorthand missives out of a deep love and respect for each other that has developed over the decades—certainly not without turmoil, pitfalls, laughable slips (right in front of the DANGER WET FLOOR sign), broken axles, lost sleeping bags and leaky roofs.

These poems evolved over several years, with a little push from friends (and publisher) these cadences are now printed and bound, more or less in their original order. Through seasons both internal and external, the idea of "book" is somewhat akin to an exhibit of paintings paired along a sunlit wall, one informing the other. Realizing that great spaces often elapsed between the writing, receiving and response to each poem, it's helpful to read them that way—in slow motion; not at expressway speed, but as if driving a country road.

(jb)

A mouse nest
in his typewriter—
that long

Let it grow all summer
a morning glory
around the rake

Sleep impossible:
crickets and
moonlight

Awakened
from an afternoon nap
by a passing cloud

At the thrift store
buying back
his own shirt

In the second hand shop
his own book
inscribed to a friend

Long after
the call to prayer
the bell rope swaying

Laid flat by the wind
autumn grass
shows the way

Admiring snowpeaks
sixteen miles
on the wrong road

Home again—
swollen rivers
and rainbows

Winter solstice:
ink drying in the light
of a faraway star

Christmas Eve:
even the bartender's
gone home

Just an ordinary day
the horse has four legs
I have two

One year
into another
no difference

An exchange of letters
no better way
to welcome the year

Six degree morning
before opening his mail
warms it in the sun

On a rainy night
a solitary chess player
in the old cafe

Last night
a house full of people
tonight the moon

Of course he says
his finest poems are in
the lost notebooks

That moment
before waking
when they all appear

Sea lions
mating in the rain
—no other business here

Morning fog
hides the vacationing couple
but not their argument

Kerouac Alley:
rotting garbage
in the air

The famous poet's grave:
ants crawling
from an empty bottle

In front of
DANGER WET SURFACE
slips and falls

Enters the sickroom
with a bouquet
taken from the cafeteria

Winter rain—
the shape of a heron
perched on a post

From the blizzard
a whisk of wings—
snowgeese

So angry
he writes off the mileage
to and from the audit

All his efforts
like grey
unmelted snow

Looking for books
in the remaindered catalog
he finds his own

His empty bottles of ink
tell him
at least he tried

Still bright
among the dry grasses
the discarded bouquet

Clinging
to the old man's umbrella
a wet chrysanthemum

A Clear Lesson Here

That hummingbird
he saved from the window
came back through the door
in the cat's mouth

Trying to get to the story
they fast forward
the pornographic video

Instead of clothes
dreams he was
trying on women

With each return
memories of dreams
abandoned long ago
—*Hollywood*

Smoke through a spiderweb:
he counts each
who shared his bed

Work cancelled
but no complaints—
a late spring shower

Clearing the table
everything
except a square of light

His thickest file reads
"Poems not Good enough
to be Saved"

Wild grasses
waving between each stone
in the abandoned pile

News of the awards
makes him smile
for a day or two

In the boat's wake
a single star
rising   falling

Only one call
on his birthday, his daughter
asking for money

What I Did at 60

Masturbated
just to be sure
I could

Not even the finest tequila
could bring her
to his bed

She's back in his dreams—
may it just be
his dreams

A fantasy realized
until he hears her say
"your generation"

A little wine
and the false humility
falls away

Long after the water's gone
I linger in the bath
—August moon

The first poem
come and gone
on the morning breeze

Outpatient surgery:
he hears the doctor ask
for a sharper scapel

Coming off the painkillers
his mind filled
with the old babble

Comet viewing—
he makes a list of where
to scatter his ashes

Getting so clear
there's nothing
to think about

Mist shrouded river:
following it
to the sea's edge

Learned a lot
hope it wasn't
too much

At the equinox
steps outside
—only the crickets

Snuffing the lantern
—a full moon
carries away the river

Reaching for
the missing handrail
night of his father's death

Returning to his father's house
he sits in every chair
waiting

Discarding
old medical bills
the tears finally flow

Autumn haze—
paying the last
of the mortician's bills

Without a sound
a moon-blue butterfly
comes and goes

Rereading his letters
table darkened
by a passing cloud

Long after
breaking the cup
still finding the pieces

With equal pleasure
he remembers those
he could have slept with

After the funeral
replacing Buddha
with family pictures

An American Buddhist dies
his family argues
about the service

Summer's end
at the door an old friend
without teeth

Realizing he has no locks
he finally throws away
a jar of keys

Over the bedroom chair
her nightgown
still warm

Because he dreamed it
the poem's never there
in the morning

So afraid
of his Halloween mask
no one comes to the door

Not changing clothes
for a week
—that kind of life

On Buying a 32¢ Stamp

What'll it be
Bugs Bunny
or the American flag?

So many letters
to answer he files
them all

3 calendars
3 different new years
none right for me

First snow—
in the clinic window
his blood in a vial

No charm
for the recent widow
—six inches of snow

Only Christmas cards
in the mailbox
—depression

No ink in the pen
he writes it
anyway

The stars' brightness
means nothing to the man
who can't see that far

Perfectly empty sky
but he fills it
talking to himself

Now and then
picks up the phone
to see if anyone's there

That cricket
finally sleeps
and so do I

Setting out—
his walking stick left
on a farmer's woodpile

Climbing the mountain
crocus underfoot
unavoidable

In the arms of the goddess
boys untangling
their kites

At the temple of Athena
church bells and prayers
from the city below

Across the river
rice harvest songs
from the forbidden country

Looking for the old places:
gone from memory
or just gone?

—*Hydra, Greece*

Pavilions once reserved
for storytellers now lit
with sitcoms

—*Ubud, Bali*

Long before the service ends
the courtyard
filled with smokers

After the ceremony
the Brahmin's offering
gobbled by the farmer's ducks

Trouble ahead—
bought my first jug
of cheap ouzo

Finishing the bottle
to the muezzin's call
on the loudspeaker

To beat the crowds
they arrive
before the gatekeeper

At the temple gate
waiting for the dragonflies
to move

Pilgrims asleep
their begging bowls filled
with moonlight

The gypsy beggar
with golden eyes—
who could refuse?

The village stream:
a boy washing his motorbike
a girl her water buffalo

In the midst
of the new
the old still calls

Forgets to cap his pen
loses
another shirt

Soaked to the bone
he begins to dance
down the trail

Joined
for breakfast
by a single sun ray

Speaks to so few
he begins
to forget how

The ferry crossing:
water and sky
becoming night

The sky   the sea
both
filled with stars

Behind the screen
a stranger splashing water
—her perfect outline

In the moonlight
on the polished floor
her naked feet

After lovemaking
smoke settling
in the moonlit ravine

Watching her sleep
he thinks: anything
anything she wants

Across the water
scattered lights
—others living quietly

Above the headlines
a butterfly
skims the rice fields

With no plans
how can he
be behind?

Over half-carved faces
the lunar calendar
in a ray of sun
—Mas, Bali

Cats sleeping
on the lit plastic Jesus
to stay warm

The butcher
huddled from the cold
between slaughtered carcasses

Mind so empty
can't even remember
his favorite jokes

Morning fog
the gong's music
suspended

"Seven University Professors
Will Be Reading Tonight"
—not to me

"The place was filled"
he brags, leaving out
there were only six chairs

"Ever popular and crowded"
but for lunch and dinner
we're the only ones

Sign in the Royal Forest

NO WEAPONS
EXCEPT THOSE NEEDED
FOR PREPARING FOOD

To three women
the same letter: "wish you
were traveling with me"

Wakes remembering
all the things
he'll never do again

One smells of musk
the other cloves
his bed of both

A Lament
Written with Relief:

None of these beauties
from foreign climes
will ever be mine again

Playground laughter
pierced by cries
from the butcher's alley

In the wake of one boat
delighted squeals
of children in another

After drinking
the waters of eloquence
his pen runs dry
　　　　—Delphi

Through spring rain
the scent
of burning pyres

Imagined camels and bears
found plastic kitchen ware
and cheap shoes
—*Ermione, Greece*

Over dusty bras and videos
the merchant tallies
his abacus
—*Varanasi, India*

Learning the trade
she limps up for alms
then skips away

No English
until a dispute
over the bill

Narcissus from the mountain
for sale
at the butcher's

The blacksmith
his ear adorned with
a red hibiscus

Poems everywhere
except where
they should be

Even in his passport
he scribbles
a few

A Letter from The Editor:

"As per agreement
  for your accepted poem
  I enclose one dollar"

Even across the seas
the rejections
reach me

Wind
or no wind
the leaves still fall

Full moon
savoring it with
an empty belly

This year
in the distance
the lights of others

In deep mist
the ancient banyan
wrapped for the new year

Never more prolific
Never so many
bad ones

At dawn trying to find
the ones lost
in sleep

At the cremation
tourists bargaining
for bone carvings

Objects not bought
regretted
then forgotten

Easter morning—
the severed fish
its head still leaping

Each in their
own plastic sack
—the bleating lambs

Instead
of moon viewing
—the design on her kimono

Finds the lost notebook
discovers
there wasn't much there

Talking of afterlife
fingers tracing
a hole in his blanket

Now with
a chance to speak
nothing to say

One of these days
one of these poems
will be the last one

A Contribution to the Understanding of the Relationship Between Buddhism and Poetry

I

I like my poems short
the shorter the better.
Not that I mind the cold
but I yearn for the sun.

II

There are few things in this world duller and more useless than Buddhist scholars and intellectuals discussing Zen practice. Surely one of them must be poets prattling on about poetics.

III

Except for Takuboku Ishikawa's dictum that:
> *The qualifications of a poet are three:*
> *he or she must be a human being—*
> *first, second, and last.*

And Andre Schwarz-Bart's suggestion that:
> *When you know that an arrow won't miss you*
> *just thrust out your belly to receive it squarely.*

I have no theory of poetics or Buddhism.

IV

Suggestions:
Read the masters.
Make it clear.
Keep it simple.

(ss)

COLOPHON

Set in *Galliard*—
designed by Matthew Carter with Mike Parker
in 1978 as an interpretation of the spirit of
17th century types by Robert Granjon.
Its dark beauty and crisp serifs have
made this one of the "new" classics
in modern typography.

●

Book design by J. Bryan

John Brandi—poet, painter, essayist, passionate traveler—
has authored numerous books and given readings worldwide.
His paintings are in international collections. Among his
honors is an NEA Fellowship for Poetry—though the "real
awards belong to the poems and paintings, not the artist."

Steve Sanfield—poet, professional storyteller, folklorist,
children's author, and ardent defender of American haiku—
has managed to pay his bills most of his life by working as
a wordsmith. His grocer and cobbler remain grateful—
as does he himself.